C000037384

The Iron Book of British Haiku

Edited by
David Cobb
Martin Lucas

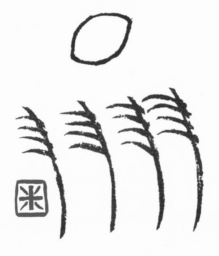

Second print 1998
First published 1998 by IRON Press
5 Marden Terrace
Cullercoats
North Shields
Northumberland
NE30 4PD
Tel / Fax (0191) 253 1901

Printed by Peterson Printers
South Shields

Typesetting by David Stephenson
and Michael Adam

Book & cover design by Peter Mortimer
Cover Artist unknown

ISBN 0 906228 67 0

IRON Press books are represented by
Signature Book Representation
Sun House
2 Little Peter Street
Knott Mill
Manchester
M15 4PS
Tel (0161) 834 8767
Fax (0161) 834 8656
Email signatur@dircon.co.uk

Introduction

This anthology has a simple aim: to present the best work of British haiku poets writing in English and Scots. A few of these poems were written a long time ago, in haiku terms – back in the 1950s or 60s – but the majority are from within the past seven years. The interest in haiku that had previously been smouldering flared into life in 1990 with the foundation of the British Haiku Society. One early BHS initiative was a collaboration with IRON Press to publish a small collection which was to become, for this country, the first widely-available showcase of current haiku practice. Over 5,500 submissions were received and the best – half of them by poets from outside the UK – were put together in *The Haiku Hundred*, now into its fourth print.

Since that collection is still available we decided not to recap any of its contents here. Our primary sources were the journals devoted to haiku which have been founded in recent years: the BHS's own *Blithe Spirit* (1990-); *Haiku Quarterly* (1990-); *Bare Bones* (1992-1994); *Time Haiku* (1994-); *Presence* (1995-); and *still* (1996-). In addition we include some poems by British writers which first appeared in magazines published in continental Europe, North America, Australasia or Japan, which were entered with success in various competitions at home and abroad, or which were taken from the ever-widening range of personal collections. Some poems are new work, appearing here for the first time.

The earlier history of haiku has been well

documented elsewhere. Briefly, it was born out of collaborative linked poetry in medieval Japan; brought to perfection by the restless *samurai*, Basho; and eventually christened *haiku* by Shiki in the last century when the genre was already 400 years old. After Shiki, haiku divided into two branches; the followers of Takahama Kyoshi respected the ancient formal conventions; the radicals of the New Trend movement didn't. The rise of haiku in English has also been charted thoroughly. A taste for the terse and imagistic was cultivated by such as Ezra Pound and William Carlos Williams; and the aspiring mystics of the Beat generation fuelled their enthusiasm with a strange brew of jazz, psychedelics and a customised conception of Zen.

What is less well known and talked about – and here and now must be a good time and place to mention it – is the aspect of haiku which strikes an oddly familiar chord to the British (as distinct from 'English-language') ear. Ancient Welsh and Irish poets made impressionistic sketches of Nature which create an uncanny quiver of recognition in anyone attuned to haiku. The parallel with Japan – no hint of a direct transmission either way is implied – was made explicit by Stephen Gill in his programme, *The Half-Said Thing*, broadcast on BBC Radio 3 in September 1994. Seamus Heaney has memorably emphasised the point, describing this pithy indigenous method as "discovering, to one's surprise, little jabs of delight in the elemental".

The love of landscape evident in these old poems resurfaced centuries later with the Romantic movement and was the heart of

Wordsworth's poetic manifesto. One defining characteristic of Wordsworth's attitude to literature is strikingly reminiscent of Basho: 'Let Nature be your Teacher'. Unfortunately (from a haiku point of view) Wordsworth's chosen forms were often more suited to expressing the grandiose and theoretical than the succinct and particular. Those fleeting moments identified as 'spots of time' were perhaps done better justice by writers who were more content just to jot and scribble: as in the nature notes of Gilbert White and John Clare; or the visions of Richard Jefferies. But even for these authors writing seems to have been a contemplative and solitary pursuit. Only now, in the earthshrinking 1990s, has haiku given us a tongue to express, share and pass on these ancient intuitions.

Two British writers prepared the ground for the acceptance of English haiku in the 20th century. Arthur Waley's lucid translations made many Chinese and Japanese classics accessible to English readers. R H Blyth provided the bulk of the earliest translations of classical haiku into English, many of which have yet to be bettered, and we include some of these here. The British Haiku Society reactivated Blyth's influence by publishing a selection from his critical writings, *The Genius of Haiku*, in 1994. Blyth's interpretation of the spirit of haiku is both energetic and idiosyncratic, relying on a paradoxical logic that is characteristic of haiku; so alive and engaging it seems irrelevant to ask whether it is 'true'.

So much for how haiku got here. What is it? In Japan, a haiku is a short poem, in the present tense, typically with 17 syllables to a pattern of 5-7-5, including some brief (often oblique) reference to the season of composition. It has been said that haiku "connect human nature with Nature" but this sounds dangerously as if they are meant to provide some sort of social service when their purpose is, as with most poetry, pure enjoyment (in the profoundest sense). So it would be more accurate to say that haiku are written from a mind-set which takes it as axiomatic that both Nature and human nature rest on one reality and that either can be used to express insights into the other. Natural imagery, in itself, can be poetry and needs neither explanation nor justification. It is the image, the concrete noun, with all its kaleidoscopic implications, which is at the centre of haiku.

How the poet attempts to follow this lead in English is a matter of personal taste. The 5-7-5 syllable form has a rhythmic beauty in Japanese and, like the couplet in English, can be employed in adverts or public notices as well as in poetry. Some English poets choose to accept the discipline of this borrowed formal restriction; others regard it as irrelevant. The seasonal flavour is less easily abandoned. Any image grounded in Nature, and many images derived from Culture, will tend to evoke one season rather than another. For British poets in particular, since we share a national meteorological obsession with the Japanese, being like them on islands exposed to winds and waves, the seasonal aspect of haiku is a resource it seems appropriate to employ. As for the present tense, it has impact and implies involvement. Not, for the haiku poet, the security of a protected vantage point, surveying the wreckage of a cultural or individual wasteland. Even in a storm, a haiku poet is part of it and does not speak against it; either we celebrate, or we shut up.

Given that haiku in Japan is prone to undergo periods of deconstruction and reinvention, and that haiku in English is still in its infancy, it is to be expected that arguments will continue as to what form it should take and how best to apply its insights. When all is said and done, there is no definition like the doing of it. These pages, containing the work of seventy-one poets, suggest the considerable diversity of approach and content that we may recognise as haiku. Each of us differs as to what attracts our attention in the first place and what colours or rhythms we use to express it. Tito (Stephen Gill) uses an expansive four lines, attempting to be as exact as possible in identifying the special quality of a particular moment. Brian Tasker and Ken Jones are more clipped and minimalist, more welcoming to ambiguities, using formulations which have a ring of 'eternity' about them. Cicely Hill and George Marsh offer vibrant tones, rich textures. Susan Rowley and Michael Gunton use a plainer language to express an inherent significance in the everyday and apparently insignificant. Annie Bachini asks us to notice and accept what we habitually exclude. Hamish Turnbull uses a quirky humour to subvert commonplace experiences. None of these 'ways' is a closed compartment and there are times when we all do all of these things.

We aim to show that haiku is not a paradise island cut off from the rest of poetic civilisation. For this reason this anthology contains examples of related genres: *senryu, renku (renga), haibun, rensaku* or haiku sequences, and haiku-influenced poetry. *Senryu* is a poem on the same pattern as haiku, without the seasonal reference, usually presenting a wry look at human behaviour. The senryu are sprinkled haphazardly throughout; haiku and senryu frequently merge in English and a strict demarcation is impossible to maintain. We have room for only one *renga*, of 36 links. A renga is a connected chain of haiku written in co-operation by a group. The process is as important as the product, but the example given maintains a high standard both in terms of individual stanzas and the linking. *Haibun* is an amalgamation of haiku and prose, sharing the haiku angle of looking at the general through the particular, with some haiku-like quality of condensation in the prose style, and incorporating at least one actual haiku. Our example is by Bill Wyatt, who finds haiku connections in the tangible remains of ancient Greece. In addition to several haiku sequences, we also include three poems built out of haiku-like units. We hope that these will serve as examples of ways in which the Eastern and Western poetic traditions might be bridged, so that traffic and influence can flow in both directions.

We emphasise that this selection is retrospective, covering a wide range of styles but not all possible experimentations. (Some may think us particularly hard on poets like Wendy Cope's Mr Strugnell. We also do not deal in 'Spam haiku'!) Through its publication we would seek to influence, but not to limit, the direction of future haiku development. We would like to thank all the poets represented, for permission to print their work and for their goodwill, which has made the task of compilation so much easier than we imagined it would be. We append a brief bibliography, which will serve as a rough guide to haiku history to date.

Martin Lucas and David Cobb
January 1998

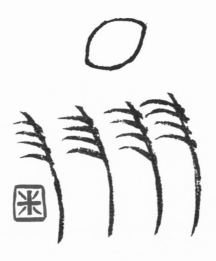

the British Haiku Society can be located at
Sinodun
Shalford
Braintree
Essex
CM7 5HN
Tel 01371-851097

Compilers' Note.

Why Scots and not other 'dialect' poems?
Though not Scots ourselves we think that
Scots is no more a dialect of English than
English is a dialect of Scots. In the Lowlands it
has a long pedigree as a literary language. At
the same time to include Scots haiku fits in
with the principle that haiku should be
written in the language the poet uses every
day. Perhaps most appealing of all, Scots is a
language full of pithy words strong on
onomatopoeia, words that stir the senses with
their earthiness, hardness, colour, lilt and
pungency – just the sort of words that work so
well in haiku.

Scots haiku are therefore not only an
essential part of the range of British haiku but
excellent exemplars of some of the qualities of
good haiku. To aid the reader unfamiliar with
Scots, an English version of each Scots haiku is
given in the appendix.

Select Bibliography

Haiku Society of America, *A Haiku Path*, HSA,1994.
R H Blyth, *The Genius of Haiku*,
British Haiku Society, 1994.
Cor van den Heuvel, *The Haiku Anthology*,
Simon and Schuster, 1986.
William J Higginson, *The Haiku Handbook*,
Kodansha, 1985.
(ed.) James Kirkup, David Cobb, Peter Mortimer,
The Haiku Hundred, Iron, 1992.
Makoto Ueda, *Matsuo Basho*, Kodansha, 1982.
Makoto Ueda, *Basho and his Interpreters*,
Stanford University Press, 1992.
(tr.) Kenneth Hurlstone Jackson, *A Celtic Miscellany*,
Penguin, 1971.

Seventy-one Poets

Barry Atkinson

Through frosted glass my visitor crying

•

spots of caviar
stain the tuxedo
of the honoured guest

Annie Bachini

after dad
tidies her scarf
the toddler fixes it herself

•

summer breeze –
the long drapes
don't move an inch

•

behind drawn curtains
distorted shadow
of a falling leaf

•

in my childhood bed
the rattles of passing trains
echo round the room

•

winter rush-hour
rebounding from the pavement
illuminated rain

•

next to the poster
'Strike Against Stress'
fish in a tank

Kevin Bailey

Hare

I found the
severed head
of a hare,

staring a dry stare,

and gobbling flies
in the long grass
by the river:

the passing shiver
of charnal Nature
closing tired eyes.

<u>Norman Barraclough</u>

overgrown garden pond –
the old stone philosopher
staring back

•

through falling snow
hillside house lights
the hoot of an owl

•

clink
of my fork striking flint –
its shortest prong

Kathleen Basford

October maples –
through so many colours
so much light
(Ontario)

•

pigs' noses
poking through the orchard gate –
longer and longer
(Lincolnshire)

David Bateman

The guest who won't leave:
smoking your cigarettes, and
missing the ashtray.

•

As each snowball hits,
we laugh like overgrown kids,
taste snow on our lips.

Sheila Glen Bishop

Remembering
last summer's infidelity:
your tongue in my cheek

Colin Blundell

in the Tate café
all conversations include
spacious hand movements

•

a short-lived affair –
the second glance of a girl
on a passing boat

•

dressing carefully
for a solemn occasion
I forget my flies

•

the autumn evening
filling the railway carriage
with a dug beet smell

•

at odds with myself –
not having bought a ticket;
the misty sunrise

at the funeral
the little bird tap-tapping
outside the window

•

the corpse is covered –
its nose makes a small mountain
in the smooth white sheet

•

raking grass cuttings –
the beautiful girl asks if
I'm ever depressed

•

management meeting –
out of the window the gulls
take flight together

•

conversation palls –
my eyes follow a spider
crossing white damask

R H Blyth

(translations of haiku by Japanese poets)

Ill on a journey:
My dreams wander
Over a withered moor.
(Basho)

•

With every falling petal,
The plum branches
Grow older.
(Buson)

•

Wild persimmons,
The mother eating
The bitter parts.
(Issa)

•

Even to the saucepan
Where potatoes are boiling, –
A moonlit night.
(Kyoroku)

•

The bright moon;
No dark place
To empty the ash-tray.
(Kyoshi)

David Burleigh

Creeper already
two more yards across the wall –
working in the heat

Brian Cater

Spring floods,
kingfisher hunting
along the road

•

After the last firework,
a shooting star

Tessa Rose Chester

hot afternoon –
the cat's tail
flicks bare skin

David Cobb

children panicking
out of the tiger cage
    a wasp

•

birthday dinner –
lid of the ricepot
bubbling over

•

drip by drip
the moonlight lengthens
in the icicle

•

a moment between
lighthouse flashes
cold smell of fish

•

daffodil morning –
looking for something
very blue to wear

•

evening by the river,
red-painted toenails
sinking into silt

•

in the draughty porch
during the committal
glow of cigarettes

Geoffrey Daniel

on the axe-head
        the smell
   split
out of the kindling

•

drawing curtains
     past the old zither;
frost in the air

•

  in between showers –
      beginning again
the patient settling of mud

•

August heat:
   erratically
      the crack shots
of the pods

•

  a bitter rain –
two silences
beneath
the one umbrella

Adele David

Afternoon garden –
autumn sun on needle and silk
travelling through velvet.

•

sun so hot –
the sound of snails
falling from walls
behind the ivy

•

first snow on Hampstead Heath –
two dogs in jumpers
with the sleeves rolled up

Roberta Davis

Under
a blazing sky
roughness of cornstalks

•

4 o'clock
Assam tea
from a leaking pot

•

Perfectly still
in the falling snow
grey heron

•

Half open door
in a wedge of light
black cat washing

Patricia V Dawson

After the operation,
she edits her symptoms
for the family

•

Ice on the front step –
two men slip as they bring in
a new fridge freezer.

Frank Dullaghan

on the teacher's apple –
small teeth marks

•

cross-roads
the fallen signpost points
at the cloudy sky

•

only myself
in the train window
these dark evenings

•

the rolling sea –
from the edge of the sky
to my feet

•

in the trouser press
my son's school tie
still knotted

Dee Evetts

morning sneeze
the guitar in the corner
resonates

•

custody battle
a bodyguard lifts the child
to see the snow

•

summer's end
the quickening of hammers
towards dusk

•

thunder
my woodshavings roll
along the verandah

•

damp morning:
cash for a journey
warm from the machine

friends from the south –
a great bowl of strawberries
in the midnight dusk

•

shaped by rock
the tongue of lakewater
shaping the rock

•

how desirable
in the thrift store window
my old Mah Jong set

•

first week of chemo
he shaves his head and buys
a jaunty cap

•

immigration
trying again to fingerprint
the old carpenter

•

in from lawnmowing
he trims his chest hairs
with the kitchen scissors

•

frozen laundry
I bend her skirt
over my arm

•

we drift downstream
his bald head somewhere
among the peeled logs

•

after the rain
on my vegetable patch
a new crop of stones

Michael Facherty

the heat of the sun
on the pool herding goldfish
into our shadows

•

in the room two flies
circling the argument
about poetry

Janice Fixter

caught in a storm
wearing nothing waterproof
except mascara

•

a final insult
on the worst day of the year –
the corkscrew's broken

Katherine Gallagher

Winter solstice:
the darkness closes in
against the church bells

•

spiderweb thread –
I walk through it unthinking
two days running

•

in the park
almost overnight,
almond-blossom

Edward D. Glover

On the great penis
of the fertility god
snow accumulates.

•

An adder glides away –
the air is suddenly sweet
with violets.

•

daybreak and frosted fields:
the brittle calls
of half-awakened birds

•

nothing precedes
six footprints in the sand
nothing follows

John Gonzalez

moonlight
a weight
on the old horse's back

•

in the village
the madman who knows nobody
is known to all

Richard Goring

March wind –
the cat teeters
             on the trellis

•

Remembrance Sunday –
         only the faint rumble
of a distant train

•

l i n g e r i n g
in the subway rush
     her perfume

•

seafront stroll
tiderush and traffic
coming and going

Caroline Gourlay

Intensive Care (a haiku sequence)

how the dark persists –
trying not to remember
your exact words

behind closed eyelids
but your smile
has come too

dreaming
the drenched sheet –
waves breaking

*

empty room
growing emptier
as the sun rises

I drive to the hospital
in my husband's car

bare ward – no flowers
your shoulders whiter
than I remember

white viburnum
against the leaden sky
a snow shower

*

trying to catch sleep –
all night the wind
circles the house

not hearing what I'm thinking
you turn the page ...

so still
after the storm
somewhere
your breathing

wind through the wires
no sound in the photograph
– spring

*

a bluetit hops
from twig to twig
– hospital garden

intensive care –
out there snow
cut off by
snow

your waterglass
I drink from it
loneliness

*

writing at night
snowflakes touch the ground
and melt

owl calls to owl –
one tree
then another

quietly
without saying goodbye
light leaves the room

*

by the open grave
sun whitens
a holly leaf

at night
the moon wanders
from room to room

enclosed pool
rocking the white sky towards me
an ash leaf.

Michael Gunton

after the crash
the doll's eyes
jammed open

•

between the bars
of the death row cell
the man in the moon

•

the snow melts
and slowly names reappear
on the war memorial

•

summer breeze
the mountain's reflection
laps at the shore

•

at dusk
the darkness between the ivy
and the wall

•

shining
in the bauble
the dog's nose

•

waves crash
against the fortifications
dead of night

Jackie Hardy

lighting the fire –
those first flames
catching last year's news

•

through stained glass
sunlight rainbows
the mongrel's coat

•

in a bookstore
two flies settle
on a romance

•

morning exercise –
blackbird on the lawn
stretches a worm

•

low tide –
to and fro in the pool
frisbee reflections

Making Sense (a haiku sequence)

across the meadow
  wind ripples the grasses
        warm breath on her neck

summer's first rose
  inhaling the bouquet
        of his sweat

sea spray
  veiling the cliffs
        salt's tang on her lips

from a glass vase
  a fall of wisteria –
        low sound in her throat

spring dawn –
  his withdrawing member
        still glistening

Seamus Heaney

Dangerous pavements.
But I face the ice this year
with my father's stick.

Claire Bugler Hewitt

Eight Weeks (a haiku sequence)

a positive result
from the pregnancy test –
trout-splash in the stream

seen from the window:
distant fields – white birds
circle in the rain

tumuli skyline –
the first pains
of miscarriage

daffodils
in a window sill–
behind them the rain pours

strange bird
with a red breast
I have not seen you before

at dawn
above the snowdrops
rooks stir

first rain, then sun –
now the sound of dry leaves
blown along the road

morning sickness –
in the wet garden:
apple blossom

Cicely Hill

Summer downpour
Green quinces lie
    Pitted with gravel

•

Embers die
The chair where the friend sat
    Fills with moonlight

•

Nudged by rain
Yew berries shift and roll
    Along a tombstone

•

At the window:
The earth drawn inwards
    This still night

•

Moving house
I pretend this stretch of river
    Is the one I dreamed of

•

This east wind day
My soft wool shawl
  Smelling of Africa

•

The fortune teller
At the fete this year
  Offers therapy

•

The first chill night
A mother finds herself
  Covering up the dolls

•

Through the storm
Hoofs of a yearling mare
  Echo thunder claps

•

Wings rustling
A dragonfly alights
  on the baby's warm head

•

Up above the lake
Where the knapped flint was found
Let's not search today

•

Autumn night:
White mist, nothing else
Out there

•

Pausing to watch
Breeze over the hayfields –
Forgotten names

Byron Jackson

early morning stillness
i chop wood
between the echoes

•

hot summer day
the long walk home
lagging behind my shadow

•

everywhere
in the garden
three white butterflies

David Jacobs

Son Rising

6 a.m. Over the bars
Of your cot your face
Rises like the sun.

●

Here, on the fourth floor,
The vending machine works
Harder than I do.

Pamela Johnson

When the light goes on
the fragile legs of craneflies
dance on the ceiling

Ken Jones

Cold tea
in a cold cup
paperwork

•

After months of rain
surprised
by my shadow

•

Washing my shirt
in the swollen river
a new year

•

out in the cold sunshine
planting early potatoes
uncertain who I am

•

By fading torchlight
squeezing out
my last toothpaste

•

Winter evening
nothing to add
to a day
which had nothing to say

•

in pale Christmas sunshine
waving   across
our disputed boundary

•

compass needle
flickering
forest silence

•

tea and cake –
my change
on a warmed saucer

•

Wandering light-headed
through the rain
nibbling Fairy Nipples

Mimi Khalvati

I climb the noon-day
peak: a broken flip-flop thong
flutters at my feet.

•

Half-standard, taller
than my daughter, her apple
buds half-green, half-pink.

Anthony Knight

Where Art and Nature Meet

Fluttering madly
a butterfly hits the path
a wasp on its wing.

I am mending a puncture
in an inflatable whale.

I brush off the wasp
from its mistaken flower
and both fly away.

The whale is slowly shrinking
as air escapes with a hiss.

Bruce Leeming

Evening – the silent
perpendicularity
of laburnums

•

Under pink almonds
eating
pink coconut ice

•

I' the snawie wynd
a chitterin gangrel:
lums reikin

•

Doon amang the birks
linties blithely jink:
cluds ahin the ben

•

Graybacks
loupin slee:
hoo quait the sprots!

•

Hogmanay splore,
bauld hechts: the morn
mair weet

•

Nune, cushie-doos
croodlin: he hauds the kame
o his deid wumman

•

Birlin doon
the rowth o gean blume
taigles a bummer

(see Appendix page 108 for English
versions)

Richard Leigh

In the crisp-packet
a blue paper twist of salt:
the night sky, the stars.

•

Mixed up in my dreams
the slam, slam of loose windows
in the empty house.

Lesley Lendrum

in the thick-rimmed cup
where the ash has lost a branch
a tiny wild rose

Martin Lucas

morning mist
a workman whistles
no particular tune

•

from leafless trees
crow follows crow
into a cold wind

•

summer's end
the ice-cream van
plays 'Greensleeves'

•

Immigration Office –
net curtains billow
with the southerly breeze

•

mumbled thanks...
on the beggar's palm
a coin-sized callus

•

hitting the shuttlecock
fly on her thigh

•

silent retreat
nothing on TV
but my own reflection

Alan Maley

When the storm has passed
We buy rain-soaked rambutans,
Full of drowning ants.

•

Our old charcoal grill,
Still cradling last year's cold ash –
A sudden shiver.

•

These chestnut floorboards,
Worn to a dark mirror
By the feet of ghosts.

George Marsh

gnarled love-signs
cut through the bark
in the year of my birth

•

in the Rose Garden
a man I don't much like
enjoying the sun

•

missed it
the moment to join in the laugh

•

stars fill the hatchway
swaying
to the smell of melon

•

summer's end nears –
now the slow bee allows
stroking of fur

•

on a rusty buoy
the fog bell feels
each melancholy wave

•

sound of dance-music –
the last fishing boat
throbs into place

•

held still
in the blur of wingbeats
the kestrel's eye

Linda Marshall

two cartoon characters
their thought bubbles are filling
with the warmth of tea

•

clock ticking:
somewhere between midnight
and the train to Leeds

Stewart McGavin

twa scarts jist a fit
abune the skinklan watter
flee intil sundoon

•

i the gloamin
twa men fae the sea
fecht on the saun

•

outby i the field
the geese sound wi thir lang craigs
dancan thegither

(See Appendix page 109 for English versions)

Matt Morden

on our backs
a shower blown
from the waterfall

Chris Mulhern

last night's rain
cupped
in an upturned leaf

•

a bucket clanks...
footsteps
and the farm falls silent

•

her reading:
a teasing breeze, lifting
a few strands of hair

Colin Oliver

A grey morning
     ducks whistle down
to skid on ice

•

In the tunnel
     the black taxi roof
     a stream of neon

•

In honeysuckle
     over the blackbird's nest
       the mother's eye.

Heatwave

Past the stone
where the lizard plays dead
I see myself gone

nettles puff seeds like smoke
the snake slips into reeds

and the elder
in the hedge runs
wild with berries

Cy Patterson

Bleak midwinter –
on the bare oak branch
a sparrow see-saws

•

Caught in a spider's web
the fly's husk
unravels

Matthew Paul

criss-crossing
the postman's path
snail-trails

•

under a lemon balm
starlit snails
eventually touch

D J Peel

the dandelion seed
on its way
to someone else's garden

•

wintry evening –
briefly the horses' breath
whiter than the moon

•

going shopping
the snail I passed
coming back

•

sea sifting back
the sky returning
with each wave

Dick Pettit

so clear –
cloud etchings on the hills
above the hills

•

the charity collector
eases open
a broken gate

•

back from leave:
new cats are pawing out
the rubbish skip

•

briefing his successor
he struggles to remember
how he did it

David Platt

in eclipse
moon still faintly visible
glaze on a teabowl

•

After the phone call
the sound of your voice ringing
in my head for days

David Purves

Scots Versions after Japanese Masters

Ma rinnie neb:
awhaur, binna on its dewdrap,
dounfaws the gloamin.
     Akutagawa Ryunosuke

•

Its sicht is tint
but for aw, for that ee anaw
A polish a gless.
     Hino Sojo

•

Strang ir the bairns
even the day ingans
daise, on the freuchie brae.
     Kaneko Tota

•

Intil ma dover at nuin,
aye an again, sumbodie
clours a nail.
     Yamaguchi Seishi

(See Appendix page 110 for English versions)

Stuart Quine

into the busker's cap
a chill wind blows
bronze leaves

•

New Year's Day...
nothing to write
but this

•

in the hospice garden
winter sun warms
empty benches

•

pulling out
her first grey hair
she finds another

•

lighting the lamp
the shadow deepens
between her breasts

Ruth Robinson

above the tree-line
only the whisper
of the chair-lift wheel

•

estuary
the artist's brush
catches the hot sun

•

telephone call
the receiver smells
of chopped shallots

Susan Rowley

growing through
the skeleton leaf –
a new year's grasses

•

loose now
on the knuckle
the thin gold

•

only the elegant angle
of a mountain brushes
the heel of light

•

shadowed porch –
a warm hay-wind moves
the unlocked door

•

kneeling
she looks sideways to see
who isn't

•

wakeful night
turning and turning
a single word

•

seedless grapes –
he spits the skins

•

two collared doves
walk circles
in the wedding rice

•

returning to
a week's emptiness – only
the dust is settled

•

in the car – finding
the distance from seat to wheel
is still yours

•

the wind chimes move –
not quite enough

Fred Schofield

old men
and sparrows
huddle

●

winter walk
holding hands
through thick gloves

●

your garlic breath
but I don't break
the kiss

●

people holding
doors open
in each other's way

●

in the overtaking car
driver and passenger
lean across to kiss

●

the size of my thumbnail
friends disappear
around the hill

•

girl with a pendant
on a long cord
bends to sweep the floor

•

bull stooping
to chew thick grass
its testicles swing

•

grassbound
in the cold wind
a feather

•

after the weight
of a hiker's boot
the tormentil springs back

Colin Shaddick

the old man says
it will outlast him
painting the rust

•

rear-view mirror
losing her
to a bend

•

the pissing horse
adding mist
to the mist

•

lightning
reveals
the staring child

John Shimmin

Invading the quay
where battleships used to berth
red valerian

•

in my diary
last week's lottery ticket
keeping my place

•

into the painting
a foraging brown insect
now ultramarine

•

this freezing night
the stillness of the stream
keeping me awake

Eric Speight

how startlingly white
the gulls are, butting into
this devilish wind!

•

Dust has collected
on her photograph but he
no longer sees it

•

the speed-boat
bounces
upon its squeal

•

Walking my friend's dog
I am shown where his mistress lives
and which is his pub.

•

All things are changing
I too change but always I
change into myself.

David Steele

as she sleeps
I watch the moonlight edge
along her thigh

•

shipping oars
I hold my breath to hear
snow on the water

•

summer thunder
wine flies persistent
at the bottleneck

•

a sudden gust
the end of season beach balls
jostle in their nets

•

Police station yard;
at the end of his tether
someone's Rottweiler

Alan J Summers

   open window
the cat dozes
   half in half out

•

*   full moon*
the hum of traffic
*   through double glazing*

Brian Tasker

heat haze   shimmering   the cyclist

•

argument over
               pushing past
the scent of her hair

•

after the birthday wish
   the smell of wax

•

high tide
over and over
the shifting shingle

•

summer storm:
on an old radio
jazz crackles

•

the house cold
after my absence
the cat sleeps closer

•

after she's gone
        unwinding
a long hair from my sweater

●

a light rain –
into the evening mist
woodsmoke

●

    in the park
a man and his boomerang
    all over the place

●

the blindman
flower by flower
smells the posy

Anthony Thwaite

(from 'A Haiku Yearbook')

February evening:
A cold puddle of petrol
Makes its own rainbow.

•

October garden:
At the top of the tree
A thrush stabs an apple.

•

November morning:
A whiff of cordite
Caught in the leaf mould.

Tito (Stephen Gill)

Wind-bells
Before the rain...
And after the rain,
Wind-bells.
  *(Shwedagon Pagoda, Rangoon,
  15.9.77)*

•

*Further down the cobble beach
The face of another
Sunset-watcher
Loses its copper glow.*
  (Northam Burrows, Devon,
  31.12.91)

•

Night wind before storm –
And coming slowly through the
trees
A white horse
Where none should be.
  (Cochin, Kerala, India, 22.3.90)

•

*The mountain
Unties my shoelace,
Throws off my staff,
Runs my water bottle dry.*
(Mottchomudake, Yakushima,
Japan, 2.8.96)

Winter evening
From the train window –
Red sun bouncing
Through a bare wood.
   *(train, between Tochigi and
   Kurihashi, Japan, 29.1.'83)*

•

*Twice the dog in the grass
Sneezes...
And once, but very loudly
I surprise us both.*
   (near Barlovento, Isla de la Palma,
   Canary Islands, 28.12.'87)

•

The man with the dragon tattoo
Old now...
And caring more
For roses
   *(Floating Market, nr. Bangkok,
   Thailand, 23.9.'77)*

Hamish Turnbull

In a crowd
the smell
of something private

•

Last night
a fog
this morning
a mountain

•

Train going south
scenery
going north

David Walker

she leaves...
a curled hair
in my soap

•

redwings feasting
beyond the chapel wall...
a Christmas wreath

•

crossing Black Mountain
wet with morning dew
black slugs.

Bill Wyatt

On Thassos – the Donkey's Back
(a haibun)

Watching the sun sink into the wine-dark sea. Centuries drifting away, along with the distant clouds. Thinking of Archilochus, that ancient Greek poet, who drank wine through a straw. Inventor of the iambus, the metrical foot. Foot soldier in the army, a sergeant – yet skilled in poetry, that lovely gift of the Muses. He gave himself the name of Cricket. Meleager called him 'a thistle with graceful leaves'. Not much of his writing has survived, fragments, scraps of paper with which mummies were wrapped and stuffed. The rest lost forever.

•

'This wheatless island
bristling with wild woodlands
like a donkey's back!'
       (Archilochus)

•

Almost a full moon
solitary cicada
prolongs my loneliness

•

A drop of ouzo
the fly dies in ecstasy –
sweet breath of autumn

Four Poets

(Fokkina McDonnell,
Stuart Quine, Helen Robinson,
and Fred Schofield)

Above the City (a kasen renga)

Above the city
the eclipsed moon
obscured by cloud

in the stone pavement
a purple flower

failing light
the logging road winds
deeper into the forest

a thin line of smoke
before the dawn

straight edge
the long horizon
draws the eye

circling the ferry
cries of gulls

across the river
shipyard cranes
summer haze

in the dole queue
his baby yawns

outside the café
giggling shopgirls
eye a taxi driver

at the opticians
he looks for the cheapest frame

her deft fingers
move the shuttle
across the loom

through the open window
piano exercises

Sunday afternoon
the steady rhythm
of the neighbours' bed

swaying on the motorway
the Blackpool coach

into blue sky
a balloon rises
above the fair

clowns on stilts
juggling with fire

the morning after
her lipstick-stained
coffee cup

over the carpet
blood and feathers

Thanksgiving
the surgeon carves
the turkey

the beggar's cap
blown away

autumn
the wind bell
never stops

stacked chairs
outside the taverna

shrieking
the blonde girl
on water skis

she lies awake
the dripping tap

eight a.m.
smoke alarm
the lodger burning toast

the infant throws away
his half-chewed rusk

long flight of the javelin
the commentator
holds his breath

pine needles muffle
passing footfalls

Christmas TV
distorted in the baubles
on the tree

on her bare shoulder
his familiar touch

stroke of midnight
we turn to kiss
the nearest face

high on the pillar
a grimacing gargoyle

peering in the mirror
the new organist
awaits his cue

out of the wind
the blind boy feels the sun

from the cool earth
a mole emerges
into bluebells

the gardener's wellies
thick with mud.

Appendix

English versions of poems in Scots

Bruce Leeming

In the snowy lane
a shivering vagrant:
chimneys smoking

•

Down in the birches
linnets happily flit:
clouds behind the hill

•

Autumn run salmon
leaping stealthily:
how still the reeds!

•

New Year party,
brave resolutions: still raining
in the morning

•

Noon, wood pigeons
cooing: he holds the comb
of his dead wife

•

Swirling down
the plenteous cherry blossom
delays a bee

Stewart McGavin

two cormorants just a foot
above the sparkling water
fly into sunset

•

in the twilight
two men from the sea
fight on the sand

•

outside in the field
the geese sound with their long necks
dancing together

David Purves

(English versions borrowed
from Makoto Ueda)

My runny nose:
everywhere except on its dewdrop
evening dusk falls.

•

Its sight has been lost
and yet, for that eye also
I polish a glass.

•

Strong are the youngsters
even on a day when onions
rot on the dry beach.

•

Into my midday nap
again and again, someone
hammers a nail.

Acknowledgements

We are grateful for permission to republish work originally published in:

Curse of the Killer Hedge, David Bateman, IRON Press, 1996;

The Desert Highway, Colin Blundell, Hub Editions, 1993;

Seeing Things, Seamus Heaney, Faber and Faber;

The Earth Drawn Inwards, Cicely Hill, Waning Moon Press, 1997;

In White Ink, Mimi Khalvati, Carcanet, 1991;

Bluegrey and *Darkness and Light*, Martin Lucas, Hub Editions, 1994 and 1996;

Salting the Air, George Marsh, Waning Moon Press, 1997;

Cloud Blunt Moon, Chris Mulhern, IRON Press, 1994;

Daisychain, Susan Rowley, Hub Editions, 1996;

Sway, Fred Schofield, Hub Editions, 1997;

Woodsmoke, Brian Tasker, Bare Bones, 1993;

Poems 1953-1988, Anthony Thwaite, Hutchinson, 1989.

IRON HAIKU

IRON Press is the most active independent haiku publisher in the country. Try our other titles listed below. Please add 70p P&P per title. Our address is on page two. Cheques to IRON Press

Jumping from Kiyomizu
by David Cobb
Illustrated by Charlotte Smith
£4.99   ISBN 0 906228 56 5
David Cobb is among this country's leading haiku writers, and this book is a life-cycle of haiku covering the gamut of human emotions, strikingly illustrated by Charlotte Smith
"A pleasure to handle – a delight to read" – Northern Review

Cloud Blunt Moon
by Chris Mulhern
£3.50   ISBN 0 906228 46 8
A highly unusual miniature book (A6 page size); a seven section sequence of haiku, each section corresponding to one phase of the moon, and the stage of a relationship. Mulhern won the 1992 James Hackett award given by the British Haiku Society. The book rapidly ran to a second print.

The Haiku Hundred
£3.50   ISBN 0 906228 42 5
This beautiful miniature book brings together 100 of the small haiku verse form, selected from more than 5,500 submitted to the anthology. The first three prints rapidly sold out, and it is now in the fourth print.

"The quality of the haiku is excellent throughout. Beautifully printed and presented" – Woodnotes Haiku Journal.

Forthcoming...

Global Haiku - Twenty-five Outstanding Poets
the most definitive world-wide haiku collection yet, gathered from throughout the English speaking world.

Out
by Jackie Hardy
a full length haiku collection from one of the North-east's most promising poets.

Both books due in 1999!